You are Flower Bloom Natashia Hagans

"Rebirth"

By

Natashia Hagans

The Story of the mind unfolding through Poetry

This book is dedicated to anyone who just wants to be heard.

Your voice matters…

Table of Contents

Introduction…

Part 1:(Painful Thoughts of the Mind)

Voiceless...

Listen to My Words You Heard….

Why Don't You Like Me…

Thank you for the Bricks…

Brother Keeper...

Manchester…

Barbie Hardly…

Secrets…

Stars…

Rejection…

Pills in slow Motion…

Part 2: (Transformation of the Mind)

Daddy's Little Girl…

Mothers Love…

Heart beats…

Guardian Angels…

Fat Girl Blues…

Rainbows and Storms…

Monopoly…

Hearts for Sale

Just Breathe…

Part 3: Rebirth: Renewing the Mind

Always be Yellow…

Committed…

Affirmations…

Lessons…

Soul birds…

Fairy Dust…

365…

My Voice…

Empire State of Mind…

Just be real…

Forever Romance…

Don't Touch My Dreams…

Shut it down…

Blessing

Golden Gates…

Issa Flower

Rebirthed

"When you change the way you look at things, the things you look at change"

"Wayne Dyer"

Introduction

This book is a combination of poems that unfolded with me as I continue to heal. During a period of my life I suffered from low self-esteem and I felt as if no one liked me. The question was did I like myself? The answer is no. I was just scared of my own shadow the news, people, and trauma crippled my existence and took me for a wild ride in my own thoughts and actions. I reached a dark place in my life where I became very nervous and suffered from paranoia. In that dark moment of my life when I wanted to give up God reached out and that's when I turned off the television and started writing. I wrote the poems for my healing I wanted so badly to have a voice in the world. Writing poems has helped me change my thought process and when I started healing my words started changing. You will catch this in the book. Meditation, affirmations, and vision boards I been doing the work so I can continue to heal. I want healing to be manifested in my life. So, come join my Journey and read my poems from a woman who just wants to be heard.

Part 1: Painful thoughts of the Mind

The mind is Fragile and other people are not always the problem. Also, as a person I'm not always the victim. Uncomfortable truths and real feelings. Come walk with me in my mind when its fragile…

Voiceless

They say you do not talk... They say speak up, they look at you in disgust... Girl or boy your roar is not strong enough...They challenge your thoughts... the voice...The epitome of soul it has joy...They say you tremble when you speak...Moses stuttered but led a nation into victory...Your words are like a whisper they say it is sophisticated all day...Impeccable and full of may like the Webster dictionary...Pause at every clause...Words so eloquent...A voice unknown the voice is so not relatable...They do not need to know you though...Your speaking abilities are poised...Do not have time to roar...This not the lion's den...Voice is the colossal of art...It comes in all forms of art...Beautiful abstracts...In addition, smooth oil paintings...On the other hand, your voice is skilled...With above average mastery...It is unique like fingerprints...Can't find in the sand... The voice is like talent... It can sing the blues...Tap dance on the moon...Balance itself out on the rope...They judge you so much...Studied you so hard...When all alone...They have no voice anywhere in your zone...So, let your voice tap dance on their souls...Push the mute button on the noise...They deeply do not want to avoid...Secretly as you talk.. they have it on speed dial...Write your own symphony...In the pages of your tear stained diary...Fill it with Drowning of words...Your voice is like a ballet...It strides in the air...It does not even blink...Your voice is like an intercom...It speaks volumes...You cannot measure it with a spoon...The voiceless has potential...Deeper than An unlocked door....The voiceless Has a voice...Stereotypes.. Do not flow...The voiceless can glide like an eagle in the sky...I mean fly very high...That voice is angelic...Like angels in heaven...It is so beautiful...It makes the golden arches break...To the voiceless...Stand tall...You are bold...Do not let anyone put you in a box...Filled with mold

Listen to My Words You Heard

Can you hear? ...Nope...Are you listening? ...Maybe... I want scream...Talking... Voice full of echoes...However, you cannot her me though...Whether I whisper or shout...You not listening to this mouth...Words so articulate...Voice is saucy...A little soft at times, they say...I dropped the mic...Because the words I say, is the truth...She speaking...Frustrated...Want to blow a fuse...Labeled as non-verbal...No, boo you just do not understand...I wonder if all creatures are created...As equals...Look to the left...Look to the right...Nothing but blank faces...Communication is not always verbal...It is a zillion to infinity of things...At this point...The way I feel to the masses...Is that I can't relate...Standing all alone...In a box...Labeled...I just do not belong...I feel all alone...Let us have conversation...It can get very deep...Take your time...Listen to me...My words are like poetry it rides in the depths of me...I need you to listen you heard...To what I say with my eyes...Body language...Not what's between my legs and thighs...Oh, no I need you to be mesmerized...As my voice rise...Do you really know me? ...I am human...I can be a teacher...If only you believe her...It seems as if I am invisible...Because of my quiet soul...Often misjudged...It's like abuse and neglect...On the other hand, even a shipwreck

Why you don't you like me?

The stank eye...The blank stare...Misconceptions of me...Now I do not care...I talk wise...A little too meek...Is that uppity...On the other hand, white talk what do you think? ...Do we bleed the same? ... Blue blood...In addition, pass smelly Gas and farts too...You think I'm a goody two shoes...No, I am imperfect...Just like you...However, by God grace, I am here to stay...I grind like you...Have no food in the fridge... Just like you...Borrowed clothes from the next because rent was due...Had my head in the clouds in school...Paid attention to few...Listen to what I wanted to...Just like you...Took my loss...From what I know...Nevertheless, I conquered them demons...And went to college though...Is it confidence you see? ...Is it all up in me? ...However, I'm scared sometimes just like you...Can't we put ego aside for a sec...Can we do things together sis...Do I intimidate you? ...You feel I can do it better...However that is all in your head as clear as this flow of rhyme...The misconceptions...Of the other...A sister or brother...One revolves around another...This sis right here wants to see everyone win...So they can feel good within...Nevertheless, a hater can rob you blind...Leave you vulnerable within...To never trust another human again...But my heart is healing...I have become me again... I will never forget the vultures I trusted from within...Life is a lesson...You definitely will get burned...But this is not a pity party...It is not my desire to keep the built up anger in my attire...I don't wonder why no more...Matter of fact who cares...It would have been a pleasure to really know me...It is too late now to show me... You do not like me is it because of my hair...Man I swear...I will smile with confidence... Because quite frankly I don't care...In the wind I go...Because people show me genuine love for sure...So stay away... I do not need the flare...The old me would wonder...Why this chic being slick...But the new me...Openly do not care so stare...However, we could have been friends though...I am not asking why you do not like me...No more...I am going to let that fly...Go ahead about your business...Girl or Boy bye...Period!

Thank You for the Bricks

Thank you for the bricks you threw…You see I am not here to fault or blame…But to say thank you…I'm not bitter or angry…Do not even need to look back down memory lane…Or should I for just a minute…So I will in order to heal…Believe me when I tell you I ain't bitter…To so many this might seem to be lame…But my memory so good when you threw them words…You see they stung me so bad…But I took the stinger out and became glad…The bricks started with words like this…Space cadet…When in reality my thought process is different from the rest…But thank you though because this was not the first brick that was thrown…Next deer with headlights…I gotta laugh at that myself…You see I'm an over thinker…Moreover, your opinion was overrated or maybe you thought I was clueless…But bottoms down I cared to much so hush…Nevertheless, thank you for the bricks stacked every word and built with it…With all the negative words thrown…Short time on earth…Words can be hard and even harder to handle from the side…Even from the top to the bottom those words hurt…But thank you though I would not have become the women I am today without those beautiful bricks…Them bricks stacked together them words…Even tried to cave me in…But I looked at them ugly disgust words and built a masterpiece with them…Those words so negatively spoken…When in reality I do not judge I try to see everyone as golden…Ask God he will tell you so…But God whispered in my ear when those bricks was thrown…Tell them thank you…For those bricks are gold…So, I thank you for the bricks they were packed with hard cement…It didn't mold me I never became hard…It helped me build a beautiful home with gold…Thank you for the bricks now I have so much strength…I might seem timid and weak…Nevertheless, I'm a lion you best to believe…Those bricks intentions were for me to fold…Instead was a glow up for thee…So thank you for the bricks yeah it was mean…Harsh and downright cold…I might have bent but never cracked in whole…However, throwing bricks back is never what I will show…Therefore, in return I have a gift…I painted those bricks with flowers…I made a name for myself it is beautiful…It has stage presence it is a flower growing from concrete bricks…Thank you for the bricks…I want to salute and give you a minute of fame for the shame you tried to brang…Yup I'm using slang and with no shame…Kisses in the air you threw those bricks, they landed, and I branded it…But to God be the Glory my story isn't over…But thank you for those bricks

Brother's Keeper

Black Male…Skittles…Young boy…Playing with a toy gun…A Gentleman…In a dark alley…A brother…Energy drinks and grind for work…A king…Running for life…Then pop, pop…He was just riding his bike…A graduate…Police called him a demon… A Young man…Holding a pellet gun in Walmart…A father…Those bullet holes in his chest is so called inflicted…A conqueror…Hustling cigarettes…College prep boy…Walking to the grocery store…A man in the mall…With his daughter…Killed by police over a scuffle…That young soldier just reppin' his hood…Fit the description of a goon…Falsely accused…The gunshots went boom boom…The young boy with the baggy jeans….Was hit during the scene…Mr. Tall…Fit the description…Of a black male hitting homes in white neighborhood robberies…Stay at home dad…Died of a heart attack while lying in bed….Police raided the wrong home instead…Homie had no funds…So he dodged a subway fare…Got hit by those bullets.. His wife cried…Because she bore his seed…Moreover, he would not be there…College freshman bought a used car…Went cruzin' on the highway…A -stolen vehicle came on the radar…Of the oppressor…Now his body lay flat…On the highways…A church boy sings hymns on his way walking home…The police told him to come here…He resisted…Got Shot once…Twice…Brother no longer here…A man with potential…With all the credentials….Walking out the club…Gets hits by the police gun…He not with us…As I type these words, he riding to his final destination in a hearse…Black Bodies chalked…On the sidewalk…Some homicides by their own peeps…Many murdered by the police…Momma weeping…Daddy want revenge…Grandma looking with her hands towards the sky…Bullets ricochet on black male bodies…Black males' body lay lifeless…They had a whole lot potential…Is that why their legacy…Has been dismantled….A genocide for decades….A target for generations…Not every brother is up to no good…Alternatively want to sale drugs in the hood…Wondering and Questioning…The loss of so many black brothers…How can I be my brother's keeper with a death for sale sign like a curse or a creeper…?

"Manchester"

I was dancing…
Fist Pumping…
Just having a good ole time…
Ariana Grande was on my mind...

Laughing with my friends…
Dressed in my best tee…
Taking selfies for memories…
Dancing side by side with my bestie…

Having no problem using my vocal at the concert to the song "Everything"
"Breaking free" to my favorite pop song by Ariana Grande…
Watching young girls be so "Focus" to listen to the ballad's old melody…
I was engulfed in the magic of the "Beauty and the Beast" …

Dancing and twerking to 'Everybody'…
As the drums went rhythm to rhythm with "Greedy" …
The pianos made its "Best Mistakes" …
I touched my tattoo as she flowed out a verse to "Tattoo Heart", the vibes were through the roof…

Then I heard a loud boom…
My bestie and I didn't know what to do...
The panic I could feel in my chest…
Anxiety had risen so I moved…

Run, run for your life in this big ole coliseum…
I watched blood drip from people's polo jeans…
Then another loud noise boom boom...
Boom Boom Boom….

The noise went through my eardrums…
Like a car engine vroom, vroom, vroom …
I smelled smoke and metal
As tripped over bodies lying everywhere…

My friends are scattered…
Cell phones shattered…
I was thinking in my mind "I'm just a kid"
It is no way I can go out like this…

I was not ready to die…
Therefore, I conquered all my fears and ran out the coliseum…
Into the cold-blooded Manchester streets…
While blood was dripping from my right leg…

But I needed to survive
You see I want to be on the stage singing sweet melodies…
Like my idol Ariane Grande …
Then I felt a touch…

I was all frightened and blue…
I looked up it was the paramedics to carry me through…
I looked up to the sky and told God "Thank you" …
Today Manchester lost young souls…
Who had potential of gold…

Others made it out of the cage of rage…
I was one of the many who survived…
Along with my besties and friends…
We agreed we would never be the same…

Went to a pop concert in Manchester came out with broken souls…

Now life as I see it will be forever different….
Some days will be blue
While other days I will be making my dreams come true…
Sing about that night that things popped off in Manchester…

Barbie Hardly

Like oh my gosh
Barbie makeup is to the gods
Weave on point
Showing them breast implants to the gram

Sparkling nails
Coconut breast shells
Body like figure 8
Foundation is flawless

Red bottoms
Stilettos'
Giuseppe's and things
Versace Jeans no knock off in between

Gucci bag
Pink diamond encrusted diamond rings
Barbie Bling
Pink Things

Poised for the camera
Diamond nails
Pearls on the bosom
Glitter scent

Filthy rich men
Bow down when they see you
They like your body
It is an addiction to them

You don't need to work
Those men hand you a duffle bag
Full of trophies
Encrusted with hella bills

But your heart is empty
With all the makeup
You feel empty
Your heart has rotted like a corpse

Without the but implants
And Liposuction
Barbie feels weird
A woman without a purpose

Looking in the mirror
Barbie Hardly is a pageant girl
A Becky
With the good hair

You stagnant even though men are attached like magnets
Not feeling whole
As you sleep
With endless men

In your mind
You don't love you
Barbie hardly
Wants a real brother

Sell the diamonds
Garnish the million-dollar homes
Without the material things
Would she be anything?

Scars hide behind the mask
Raped as a child
Became a grown up to early
Vowed to never let a man break her heart

Therefore, she chose to finesse
The money, men, and jewelry

She gave them a fake smile
Filled with foolery

Barbie hardly cries at night
Nightmares of being raped
Now cold hearted
As knife
She took her brokenness and covered it up
With beauty
A vow she preyed
To be a gold digger always

She snatched what was token
Her jewels that was scared
Therefore, she wore the Barbie hardly crown well
And snatched all the jewels and crowns

Nasty attitude
A diva and a beast
Two lethal combos
Everything selfish she wanted to be

Pink puckered lips
A crystal crown
Barbie hardly was a ruthless soul
She wanted all the men to fold

Secrets

Peekaboo…
Lurking around…
Finding shadows…
So definite those discreetly secrets…

Hush, Hush…
No one is supposed to know…
So many little secrets…
None in the treasure box for show…

Hiding behind the bright yellow sun…
So deep within the moonlight…
Trees with shadows…
Glass containers with lids secrets hidden…

Blanket over top of head…
Secrets so deep…
Secret's pedaling over…
Puddles of secrets here and there…

Like a woman with make-up…
Like a mask…
Those secrets kept within…
Water cannot hold the fire within…

Butterflies…
With no wings…
Cannot fly…
Secrets covered up, oh my…

Thoughts
In a blink of an eye…
You wonder if they know your secrets…
Even with the blinds closed…

Summer Breeze...
Writing with a flow...
Listening to the girl group Xscape...
"This is my Little Secret"...

Paranoia...
Taken a toll on you...
Because you want the secrets to be, free...
Nevertheless, it is like a caged bird who wants to sing...

Kiss and tell...
Wonder....
Traces of secrets...
Left imprints in the sand...

It sizzles...
Like a winter, freeze...
Secrets....
No souls would ever believe...

Pretty face...
Handsome smile...
Pearly white teeth...
Hidden secrets that many would be shocked to believe...

Suited up...
With a necktie...
Clean shoes...
Drink Hennessey to keep them secrets smooth...

Trickin' at night...
Sleep by day...
A secret bottled up inside...
Pop a Molly near your bedside...

Ashamed is written on your face...
Looking to ground...

Because you went down the wrong lane…
Those secrets you battle every night…

Self-whispers in ear…
Do not reveal those secrets…
Momma will not approve…
Daddy going to make you choose…

Life…
Wrapped in a pretty bow…
Mermaids and Unicorns…
Secrets wrapped in a blue tiffany box…

Merry go round…
To the horses in the back…
Trip trop…
Secrets so ugly they leave muddy trails on hearts…

Disappear in the wind…
Cannot stay too long…
Figuring me out…
Is like telling your best friends secrets…

Secrets kept in the dark…
No one needs to know
They abandoned like a lost puppy…
The sneak up sometimes…

Like the meow of a cat
Scratching my neck
Those secrets….
Hidden….

Stars

Wish upon a star
The glitz
The glamour
Fast life

Sipping thousand dollars' worth of champagne
Wearing blood bottom
Flashy
Shining bright like diamonds

But they don't know
Behind the star status
Is a bad dream
Life of a dope fiend

Snort Cocaine
To get rid of the pain
The mirrors in the dressing room
Is a way of escape from fans?

Plush Furs
Gold encrusted grillz
Fast Ferraris
Top of the line Maserati

Flashy money
Clout, clout
While popping mollies
With extra paparazzi

Living it up
Living it
Living it
Living it up

Thousand entourage
It is deep
But is fake
It seems as if the dream team can't be shaken

The world doesn't know
It is not what it seems
This is a fraud
The Beverly Hills dream

The media is paid
For the showoff
My dirty laundry
Stays in the sheets

The grind is real
But in the mind
Is being a star
Truly real

To those who want to be famous
Did you miss out?
Or did being skipped
Make you flip

Some stars just want to be average
Wish they missed the opportunity
And stayed a classic
Because Hollywood is plastic

What up with the star power
Most of the stories are Tragic
Because fake Barbie and Ken
Isn't lavish

Let me define star its lame

S is for sudden fame
T means talent that is claimed
A stands for an ambush of reality
R is Rustic the beauty of fames that fades drastically

Like the Nursery rhyme goes
Twinkle, Twinkle little star
How I wonder what you are
Up above the world so high
Like a diamond in the sky
Until the fame and glory becomes bizarre

Rejection

In my ears
All I hear is
No
No
And No

In my mind, all I can think is three
Words
No
No
No

In my heart all, I can
Feel is
No
No
No

AS I walk up the hills
The rhythm says
No
No
No

As I walk down the valley
My shoes have echoes
No
No
No

As I enter the door
My tummy growls
No
No
No

As my sweaty hands turn
The knobs
No
No
No

When I see the chair
It squeaks
With
No
No
No

The wind on the window
Pain whispers
No
No
No

The people enter the room and sit
Look with a cold stare
No
No
No

I introduce myself the vibes isn't right
I declare
No
No
No

I speak with enthusiasm
However, it feels wrong I am blown
No
No
No

You see I heard so many no's
Each one was a blow
So immune
The rejection made me feel
Low

Out of pure shock, I hear a whisper of a yes
Man I feel so blessed
I looked up
And my heart
Was at rest

This not a rejection
But a resurrection
Yes
Yes
Yes

I finally was not rejected
So reach within my soul
And sing
Yes
Yes

Pills in Slow Motion

The mind is fragile...
Thoughts a mile long...
Wondering if this and that was done right...
The mind shuts down sometimes...
Popping mental medication to slow it down...

Crazy they say...
Don't do that...
The mind sometimes does not unwind...
Thinking all the time...
It's like racing in a marathon, but you never get a baton...

It affects your sleep you see...
Those thoughts make you scream....
Insomnia is as if raindrops on your window seal...
Anxiety or Depression...
Popping pills for anxiety in slow motion...

In my head, did I do right by my dad...?
Wanted so badly to cure that sick man...
I just could not do it that stuck in the head....
Traveled many miles to show my love...
Did love reach through...?

Granny and Grandma in Heaven now...
Left this world seven month apart exactly...
My world feels under attack...
The mind keeps pacing...
The medication pills have me fading...

People's opinions of me...
Have a Sista worrying with grief...
What have I done to them that was so wrong?
Cannot stand it many times...
It makes me think of heaven being my home...

Deadlines and reflections…
A whole lot of pressure…
People bickering and flexing…
My Mind is racing…
Trying to be perfect in an imperfect world…

Bombings and False presidencies…
Black Lives Matters…
When all Lives Matters…
Revelations after revelations…
All this negativity got my mind as toxic as can be…

Television full of confusion…
The footprints in my feelings like fatal bruises…
Why my black sister and brother on attack…?
Got shot forty times
The news report this with no slack…
Life so scary…
Moms been robbed at gunpoint…
This right here puts shock trauma on the brain…
I cry out Tupac song Dear Momma…
'Cuz for real these thought in my mind is trauma to the brain…

Spoke to a shrink…
Gotta get these feeling out…
The stereo types in the black community…
You crazy for seeing a shrink…
But I have to get these feelings out while I'm popping mental pills in slow motion…

Thoughts' of suicide…
Drinking bleach would do the trick…
No slitting that wrist…
What to do…
God I am done I'm through…

Momma praying….
Prayer warriors slaying…
Breakthrough glazing…
Oh God above I thank you…
No, the death Angel did not take me…

The mind needs rest just as much as your body…
We cannot run forever…
Seeing a shrink is ok, it was the best you see...
Sorting things out in the head…
I am a witness to the test…

The struggles of life ….
Are not meant to handle alone…
We not superwomen or superman…
Talk about it and leave it on Gods Throne
It is ok to take mental pills in slow Motion…

The stereo types of crazy needs to stop…
One out of four we are on a mental block…
Stop laughing and denying…
We all need help in this life Journey…
You can call me crazy, lunatic, or deranged but I see a shrink and take mental pills in slow motion…

Got dag it I am not ashamed….

Transformation of the Mind Part 2:
"I'm thankful for my struggle because without it wouldn't have stumbled across my strength"
"Alex Elle"

Daddy's Little Girl

Metaphor of a fairy tale…

Hugs…
Kisses…
The comfort…
Before the goodbyes...

Pep Talks…
About everything…
In a little girl's eyes…
Every girl doesn't get the advantage of being daddies' little girl…

Watching movies…
Laughter and play…
Buttery popcorn and junior mints…
Every little girl dream…

My Reality of Daddy Little Girl tales…

The realization of it all is some little girls are robbed…
The dreams are not the same…
Daddy holding your hands at Sweet 16 are dreams and wishful memories….
No this is not shade…

Time flies for little girls at times…
Puberty comes so fast like the ink being written in a journal…
Some of us girls have distant relations with our fathers…
It can be strained…

Life happens there's no one to blame…
In my head, I think of the times…
You never showed up….

This is my truth....
I choose to forgive...

(Memories in adulthoods)

Later on, in adulthood, the relationship turned around...
Our future as Father and daughter got bright under the light....
Riding the bus together our spot...
It was Ruby Tuesday or P.F Chang's...

This is no bluff....
As time pass...
We became peas of a pod...
We alike...

Forget those years we missed...
I am claiming the fame to Daddy Little Girl...
Eating bubble gum...
Bringing you back freeze cups...

Later on, down the road
No more bus rides...
Your frail body...
It is scary...
But I still know you as daddy...

I visit when I can
Leaving you can be so hard...
Because the look you give...
Is "Can you take me with you?" ...

You can't go with me and you know...
I'm still your Little Girl...
Daddy's Little Girl...
Love you daddy...

You love sweets...

Late at night…
A sugar rush…
You a diabetic bruh…

Now you cannot really hear…
I have to write words on paper…
Real Big…
It written like this: **Hi Daddy**…

Always wonder if I made you proud…
Sitting at Greyhound…
Waiting for the bus…
I want to do more for you…

When you close your eyes…
Do you think of me…?
In an image of a baby girl…
Am I your world…?

I know one day we will have to say goodbye…
I see it…
In your Eyes….
Until Then…
I love you Daddy…
I know you love me so….
Daddy's little girl…

A written letter to my daddy…

Mothers Love

Lovely…
Kisses…
Hugs…
Happiness…
Unconditional…

Stern…
Provider…
Counselor…
Giver…
Life…

Role Model…
Passionate…
Survivor…
Smart…
Funny…

Incredible...
Flexible…
Inspiring…
Initiative…
Creative...

Listening…
Discipline…
Intriguing…
Exciting…
Healer…

Real...
Pleasant…
Firm…
Understanding…
Guider…

Patient...
Driven...
Empathy...
Supporter...
Beautiful...

Intelligent...
Warrior...
Fearless...
Incredible...
Queen...

A Mothers love...

Abundant
Empowering
Whole
Ambassador...
Humanitarian...

Radiant....
Poised...
Powerful...
Humorous...
Extraordinary...

Graceful...
Devoted...
Flaw some...
Different...
Kindred

Sensitive...
Superior...
Guider...
Confident...

Visionary…

Epic…
Bejeweled….
Worthy…
Captivating…
Phenomenal…

Welcoming…
Strong…
Sensitive…
Organic...
Healer...

Eccentric…
Passionate…
Trustworthy…
Different…
Splendid…

All of these words
Beautiful statements
An Epitome
Of a
Mothers Love

Heart Beats

Slow breaths...
Pulse rate...
Shallow chest rising...
Code blue is the front view...
It is the Masters' plan...
Heavens Gates await...

Love ones' crowd around...
To say their final goodbyes and take one last cry...
While the ears so delicately hear...
The I love you...
Mama I will miss you...
Daddy take care...

Before the last breath...
Memories of yesterday and years flash by...
Oh, how you remember dancing in the sun...
The monitor goes beep, beep, beep...
The last of last...
Heart beats...

Still on memory lane...
Childhood days...
Licking your favorite ice cream, which is vanilla from a cone...
Running forever in green pastures knee deep...
Only remembering the good before crossing over...
Swing from a swing in crisp air, trickling fingers through the waves on the sandy beaches during summer's vacay...

Eating peanut butter with your bare hands from the jar...
Singing gracefully...
Hearty laughter as your brother's jokes go by...
Dancing and swaying your hips to Motown's greatest hits...
Memories are flowing...
Before the heartbeat misses several beats...

The tears in your eyes when your first born took her first steps…
Your first kiss under the moon…
The way you would look at yourself in the mirror with a loose tooth...
The goose bumps when you saw your first crush…
More Memories
Still remembering before the heartbeat stop counting…

The sweet taste of jelly bellies…
Krispy Kreme donuts dripping from the corners of your mouth…
Remembering only the good things…
Because minutes are few…
Days have gone by…
Years no longer await…

Reading poetry from a book…
Blowing bubbles…
Playing in dirt…
Watching the lightning bugs glow across the crystal blue southern sky…
The small things counting on my fingers…
Heart beats fading because it's not much longer to stay…

Magical Kisses…
Listening to symphonies…
These things fading away…
Into distant memory…
The heartbeats are getting slow…
Slower, Slower…

Just a little bit more memories…
Before going into eternity…
Sliding my finger on a rainy widow seal…
Eating mommas cake batter from the bowl…
Smelling fresh flowers…
Roses, tulips, and dandelions…

Going in circles on the carousels…

So many good memories...
That be touched...
Now the hearts beats are going so slow
I mean slow...
Like a turtle going to the finish line...

The trumpet plays.
The sky opens...
While clouds separate it's time to enter the pearly gates...
The heartbeat stops as cold morning dew...
Life on the other side will be all new...
Aches and pains have no clue...

The final breath draws near...
The heartbeat stops...
A last final smile...
As heavens gates awaits....
So refreshing and new...

Guardian Angels

Believe…
Way above the clouds…
In the atmosphere of crowds…
Something so invisible but real,
Guardian Angels…

Here to protect humankind…
Everybody has one assigned…
Sitting next to during bedtime…
Guardian Angels…

A car is coming…
Something brisk moves you before it becomes fatal…
The feeling of power is standing next to you…
Guardian Angels…

Asleep and dreaming…
Then all of a sudden, you feel as if you are not breathing…
You wake up instantly, cold and full of sweats…
Guardian Angel…

Intuitions whispering….
Third eye warning
Did God send thee to remind thee of futuristic things…?
Guardian Angels…

You are beeping the horn…
So much traffic you do not want to be late for work…
Then a flash of news comes on the radio, your building crumbled…
Did your Guardian Angel help you be late…?

Look into someone eyes…
Something just does not seem right…
They do not have the right vibes…

Weeks later, you receive a proclamation that your Guardian Angel was trying to tell you boo...

A person is following you...
Panic-stricken has come across your face...
However, unexpectedly someone stands beside you...
It is no coincidence that was your Guardian Angel who came very soon...

They hollering in your face...
You about to smack a chick and put her in her place...
But a swift movement holds your HAND
Your guardian Angel makes you walk away...

Not a nickel or dime...
Starving belly in mind...
Doorbell rings...
Auntie has brought a bag of groceries...

Knife to your wrist...
You had it with life...
Cannot keep going...
But something in the atmosphere tells you no...

Sleepless nights...
Thoughts racing...
Cannot sleep it out...
Is it God waking you up because he needs your attention...?

God assigns us each a Guardian Angel you see...
Because he wants to protect you...
He does not want to leave you behind...
Therefore, he sends angels from heaven to the ground...

Fat Girl Blues

The scale
Weight overflows
Mind full of doubt
To fat
For this society
Therefore, she stays closed up in a room full of doom

Don't look good in this
Or that
Bulges hanging over
All those stretch marks
And
Belly fat

Double chin
Gluttony becomes a sin
Donuts and pastries
She does not really want it
But food
Takes the pain away and is so much delight

She tried every diet
Weight Watchers
Jenny Craig
Fasted
Almost starved
To death

Slim and fit is what I need
Skinny people can be
So mean
A myth
Put into my head
Body shaming, I am the one to blame

Every outfit
She tried on
Doesn't look good
Put the mess back on the rack
Ashamed of self
This a fat girls blues

Is it weight?
Or deeper than that
Do I like myself? She states
With droopy thighs
Baggy armpits
And so much more

Fat Girl Blues
Is it true?
We do not love ourselves
Or is disbelief
That she cannot prove
Therefore, I slam the door to my room

Fat girls do not love themselves
Is that why we hang around the shadows in deep blues
Daze in the sky
Eat everything in sight
To take way the fat girl blues

Then a light bulb goes off
She a Diva
Yes, a Diva she snaps her finger like that
Stand up tall
Let her reintroduce herself
She a bad mamma jamma

She like any other human
She going to stand tall with all her flaws
She walks the runway with all the glory

It's like telling a fat girl blues story
So do not get it twisted or confused
Her butt still fat but she doesn't have the blues

Her affirmations are written on the dotted line
She confident
Magnificent as can be
Divine
Not a perfect size
However, authentically true

Only one that can judge lives in the heavens
She made a name for herself
Got rid of stigma
Behind the
Fat girl
Blues

Rainbows and Storms

Rainbows in the sky
Red
Purple
Orange
Blue all in alignment

Gods promise tattooed across
The sky
Peace
Love
Joy
And confidence

Ambition
Sparkles
Sunshine
Glitter
Rainbows tattoos in the sky

Golden
Cologne
Hard Sweat
Masculinity
Feminist
Written in the sky

Violets
Yellow
Pink
White
Bubbles of Periwinkles
All upon a rainbow in the sky

Mermaids
Unicorns

Brokenhearted
Brilliant and mental
Innocent
A colony of rainbows shining so bright

Silver
Gold
It sparkles
So Bold
Diamond and Platinum's
Illuminate a rainbow

Thunder
Lights
Hard rain
Like tears
Drip Drop
As the thunder in the storm claps
Black within
The night
No one sees
The vision before thee
Is not clear
It's narrow and dark

The valley in the storm
Is brown
Like
Mud
It is all squishy
And slides through a grasping hand

The lightning resembles
Streaks of fading memory
It is frightening
A dark place
Like insomnia

The storm does not remember

The storm rain is crashing
On the window pain
Folks drenched
Clothes so soggy
No place to get dry
Trapped in a dreary storm
Ellipse of lighting
Bolts
Fire and heat to the earth
It is like
An
Angry and loud voice.

Storms colors are dark
Full of no hope
Memories of it ain't dope
You stay in the bed and mope

But when rainbows and storms
Mixed together
It is a great combination
Of happy and sad
Angry and fulfilled with glee

Rainbows and storms
Is like passion
Heated and aroused
Fantasies and dangerous
In the mind
It is all between

Everything becomes grounded with rainbows and storms
Especially with human beings
Makes everything complete…

Monopoly

Open Mic
Some might get mad
But it will be all right
With what I'm about to say
So I speak about it any way
Yup I speak on it

Religion is like monopoly
Which pastor can win souls today?
Baptist
Catholics
Methodist
Lutherans

The list goes on and on
Who states the scriptures the best?
Muslims
Jehovah Witnesses
Seven-day Adventist
Nondenominational who knows?

The praise and worship
AME Church
Apostolic
So many religions
But
Are they putting God First?

Jesus walked on water
Talked to the Gentiles
Pharisees
Samaritans
All outside of the church
Jesus helped feel their void

Nothing was beneath Jesus
He rode on a donkey
Washed his brother's feet
His occupation was a carpenter
He preached and taught
Outside of the four walls of the church

So I ask what is the perfect religion

They all praise and worship
The Father and the Son
Listen to Psalms symphonies
And
Melodies

Which religion is the best?
It like monopoly
Moving forward
On church glistening property
Having shouting matches
On which religion teaches about God
The best

Jesus spoke the work while riding camels
And his disciples were right on track
Makes you wonder
If religion is funny
It don't make sense
Honey

I have seen every aspect of religion
Jesus was so much more
That's why he was the greatest man
Who ever lived
Many religions have the same flavor
Just a different flow

It is so much the same
We all pray
To our heavenly father
Hopefully spread the good news
In different languages
And tunes

Religions have a lot in common
We ask God to forgive us
Of our sins
As we pray
pray
And repeat ever day

So, religion is like monopoly
Some are
Some not
Nevertheless, the motto goes like this
Universally we are all connected
Spiritually

Wanting to do right by our heavenly father
Be an example like his son Jesus
Walked the earth
Be a living example feed the homeless,
Preach and teach outside of the church walls
Do I need to drop a mic?

Nope I don't need an applause

Hearts for Sale

Real hearts
Multiple of hearts
Blue hearts
Purple hearts

Happy hearts
Pink hearts
Black Hearts
Broken Hearts

Hearts for sale
On the lawns
Sale signs
Love for sale

The price tag
No one knows
It is for sale
Like a heart shaped lollipop

Love so pure
Happy
Sad
Confused

Anger
Madness
Authentic love
Hearts for sale

Like a puzzle
Broken into pieces
Heartbroken
Tiny pieces

Hearts for sale
Putting the pieces
Back
Together again

Hearts bleeding
Boom, Boom
Palpitations
Hearts for sale

Hearts for sale
In Sync
The sparkle
The shine

Screaming
And
Yelling
Hearts for sale

Ripped apart
Confused
Tears
Stressed out

Can't hold on to it
Put up a sign
In Black and white
Hearts for sale

Kisses
Hugs
Fantasies
Desires

In the mind

Is this
Love
Or Lust

Don't have it figured out
Love is not fair
Pulling
Tugging
Vulnerability
Don't want to return
The love
Is real and raw

Love can be lovely
Love is pure
Love is genuine
Hearts for sale
On a sleeve

Just Breath

Just breath
Inhale
Exhale
Meditate
Free your mind
Just Breath

Inhale
Exhale
Meditate
Free your mind
Just Breathe
Breathe

Breathe
Inhale
Exhale
Meditate
Free your mind
Just Breathe

Breathe in 1, 2, and 3
Breathe out 1, 2, and 3
Deep breathes
Air reaches so high
High to the mountain
Comes out from the bottom of the ocean

Space between breaths
The momentum
The epitome of it all
Breathe
Relax
While taking it all into your mind

Relax for the moment
Seconds
Minutes
Hours
Days and months
Even years

Just breathe
Breathe
Inhale
Exhale
Free your mind
Just breath

Refreshing
Like Spring water
Misty like rain
Crisp like snow
Sweaty hotness
Just breathe

Breathe
Inhale
Meditate
Just breath
Breath
Exhale

One, two, three, inhale
Four, five, six, Exhale
Seven, eight, nine, meditate
Close your eyes
Dream
Just Breathe

Part 3: Rebirth: Renewing of the Mind
"You were born a child of lights wonderful secret you return to the beauty you have always been"
"Aberjghani from visions of a Skylark Dressed in black"

May you always be Yellow

May you always shine bright
Brighter than the golden gates
Let the yellow in your soul illuminate
May you always be yellow

Let your light shine oh let your light shine
That golden voice let it sing for eternity
As bright as the yellow in a rainbow
May you always be yellow?

You will always bloom like a yellow daisy
In full bloom
Or like a sunflower in a garden
May you always be yellow

Continue to smile
Smile to the golden yellow sun
Shine so bright the stars in the sky sparkle like yellow fairy dust
May you always be yellow

When you speak with poise
Or enter the throne
May your crown always glisten
May you always be yellow

May your mansion be beautiful like yellow diamonds
Rare and authentic
Never seen before
May you always be yellow

When you enter a room, it will always glisten
So delicate like a lemon meringue pie
Each bite full of you will be tasty
May you always be yellow

Let your heart overflow with yellow
A favorite color of yours
I know a color so bright
May you always be yellow

Yellow is happy
It smiles before anyone shows up
It pours down happiness in multitudes
Yellow is so phenomenal it has become a friend of mine

Yellow is mellow
A sight to see
So rare in style
Many cannot wear it or pull it off

It's phenomenal an eye catcher
It radiates within you
It's so you
What I am telling you is true

May you
Always
Be
Yellow

This poem is dedicated to my cousin Chaneta Juliet Boone

Committed

Images of dreams…
On a pedestal…
Has it reached the clouds?
Better in the heavens with the Angels…

Woke up one morning…
Committed to that dream…
I want it to go so far…
It reaches the depths of the seas…

Be so committed…
That your dreams come true…
Root that dream like a seed…
Wrap it up with soil…

Water your dreams let it breathe…
You see it will forever bloom…
Because it could never be doomed…
You are so committed…

Like raindrops falling from the sky…
Or the eagle flying high…
That dream is so relatable…
The textbooks could not make it debatable…

It is so fresh to death…
That dream is so committed…
It is better than living in Bel Air…
'Cuz Fresh Prince cannot compare…

Dude hold your crown…
Sis the president salutes you when you come around…
That dream so genuine that it leaves trails of footprints behind…
Yeah you so committed…

Dreams of selling spices…
Imagine being a writer, poet or blogger…
A scientist, mathematician, or engineer…
What is on your mind something so committed it better than latest iPhone
no human will be able to resist…

Committed to that invention…
Smell the newness of that billion-dollar property investment
You just sold…
It was your best intentions…

Many will not be able to relate to your dreams…
Because at your rate…
It will be so profound…
That you will taste every consonant and vowels from the word
committed…

Love the idea of having a dream like Martin Luther King…
Invest it with no rush…
That dream is so real…
Climb up the ladder with Ribbons and bows touching the skies…

Dream of a nail salon…
Yes, it's on and popping…
Open that nightclub with the smooth marble floor…
As the deejay is celebrating the mystery of being committed…

Let everybody know that your dream is not for sale…
It is red as fire like a corvette…
The details are better than a Porsche…
That dream is so committed it is going splash, splash at the car wash…

Sprinkles on the cupcakes…
Everything you have dreamed of has your logo and design…
Oh, that cupcake business is called "Heavenly Divine" …
When they taste that lemon moist cake you just baked, they know you was
committed…

Sing like a hummingbird…
Girl you had better sing that dream…
The streets are saying you so committed…
Your voice cannot be boxed it holds volumes without a cost…

Committed that word is so long…
It is like a flower…
Or a ballet dancer who taps…
Either way it's going to bloom…
If you water that dream every day, it will make its way…
Once you are committed, it leaves a spark and have the potential to be groomed…
A little fairy dust shields that dream…
One effort makes an empire…

You see that empire becomes monumental because it is so committed….

Affirmations

Affirmations are like silhouettes...
It holds potential it stands out...
Every word comes from the heart...
It sticks to the core of the soul...
It has presence in the moment like mindfulness...
Affirmations are like tunes to a piano with notes...
You could be drowning inside...
But the words that come to life while you write make you float...
The words can be long or deep...
Or short and sweet...
Waves in rhythm...
The pace of a heartbeat...
It is refreshing as delicate tea...
Writing them down or paper boost self-esteem...
Wise words....
Affirmations are definitions to soul beats...
Gazing in the sky the affirmations is in alignment with the sun...
A glorious gift of words...
Settling in the dust leaving prints...
Because it is you that it has touched...

Lessons

Life lessons
Like pages in a book
Torn and withered
Pages, chapters, trilogies
Lessons
We all learn

Hurts and struggles
Happy and sad days
Peaks and low blows
Pearls of wisdom
Blood and thorns
Lessons of life

Good and bad
Scars and scratches
Sunshine's and rainbows
Misty raindrops and drastic measures
In the end when your last breath runs through
It all amounts to beautiful lessons

Soul birds

Soul birds
The feeling of togetherness
Their souls are wholesome and equates unity
Soul birds in harmony
They gather no friction or animosity
Only uplifting sweet melodies
Soul birds tweeting
Souls breathing
They have no plots or twist
Just every human beat in alignment
Soul birds sitting near a tree
Looking to the stars
They are one
To heavenly tunes

Fairy Dust

Dim the lights
Her shine glitters like his
The stars make them one
Sprinkle the fairy dust

He walks with confidence
Across the stage
She struts down the runaway
Like a model

He is smiling
She is beautiful
The twinkle in her eyes as she gazes in his eyes
Reminds her of shimmer and fairy dust

She walks like a boss
He suited to the tee
Their confidence shows when they speak
They both dripped in fairy dust you see

Couple goals
She walks behind his masculinity
They in formation
Drumming roll call to each other's beat

With fairy dust, they are complete
Shine bright like a diamond
Both seem ruff and tuff
Both are inferior
It in the DNA interior

He a wild factor
She spits beats
Both make millions

To golden fairy dust beats

She has a little girl smile
Can dance and flex like a ballerina
He prays for their destiny
Drop down to the pulpit at the drop of a knee

His desire
Is for both of them to get better in time
Just like fine wine
With such fire

A beautiful bond they have this couple
The kisses they give each other is magical
They sprinkle it like shimmer
And fairy dust

The goals they have are like soaring eagles
It is so high in the sky
Where dreams belong
Like a choir singing from the mountain top

They both have a wish
She thought of it first
To build an empire
He blew fairy dust on it and made a wish

They have a daughter
They both hold her small hands
Because they want her to have angel like plans
So, they pray with her every night

You see this is black love
They wake up every day and pray
Get out of bed
With hopes and fairy dust dreams

Fairy dust sprinkled is all up in their home
It is real
No one can break the bond
This couple sprinkled their dreams

On a merry go around
That goes around and around
They don't let it die
It is a dream they have let fly

365

One-half of a second
Seconds
Minutes
Several minutes
One hours
Several hours

One day
Four days
One week
Many weeks
One month
Twelve months

Have you done anything?
Yet
One year
Two years
Three years
Have you accomplished your dreams?

Five years
Ten years
Did that dream fade away?
Wrote a book
Open that business
Become a motivational speaker

Twenty years
Built that business
Built that brand
Become a Mogul
Forty years
Have you made a future?

365 days of a year
Breath
Inhale
Exhale
Release
Have you run into your destiny?

The time is ticking on the clock
Tick tock
What are you doing
Are you stuck and stagnant?
Not moving
Slowly killing your dreams

Run the race
Not for perfection
But progression
Choose to smile
With all your struggles and doom

The year is still here
What have you accomplished?
In your new year's resolution
Is it dusty?
Like a shelf
Hasn't been wiped down in years

Now is the time Kings and Queens
To position your crown
Become royalty
All the folks
Were chosen to sting like a bee

Every second counts
Every minute awaits
Every hour is an opportunity
Every year

Is a time to handle
Your fears

Believe in the seconds
Make goals in your minutes
Write them down for many hours
Every day roll up your sleeves
Do what God put you here on earth to conquer
Every Man and woman
Boy, girl and child
Rise to the occasion
Make it happen
You will be surprised

Put these words on ink
Three hundred
Sixty-five
Days
Out of the year
To be great over and over again

Humanity

Races of all kinds
Living together…
No Division
Or injustice

Hate is the past
United in the sun glaze
Black and whites
Reds and Browns

Joining together in harmony
Voices heard
Protesting is often unheard
Tears of joy

Homeless and poor
Rich and the Middles
No more slums
The ghetto is not no more

Food is abundant
Clothing is affordable with no labels
Conversations are negotiable
With no deceit

Prison doors no more
Drug addicts do not roam
The streets
Doctors, lawyers, and teachers are attainable without a degree

Healthcare is not a joke
Grandma can freely get a scan
Diseases do not exist

Grocery stores looks like

Beautiful murals
All are welcome
Come take an apple, banana, orange, or pear

The oceans water is glistening
It is clear
All creation dancing
Of dreams of sweet liberty

Fourth of July fireworks is real
Everyone is free
Politicians do not lie
They actually keep the earth safe

Parades in the streets
Every race
No one put to the side
A whole lot of human pride

Every race chuckling and jiving
With the masses
All animals
Sitting in a magical tree

Hip Hop Blasting in the air
Salsa and country playing to
Everyone dancing to rhythm
And Blues

The news is happy
No wars
Only love
And new hair grease

No Pollution on Mars
The world is full of beautiful stars
Minds have solutions

Views like staircases

Stray animals are not beaten and bruised
They roam around
Like humans
With carefree

Children of all colors
Play
In tree houses and chalked
Sidewalks

Money is not a trade
Things are freely given away
Injustice is very far
Peace is written in graffiti on the walls

Religion is for all
Baptist, Jehovah Witness, Catholics, Muslims
Holds hands and will not fall apart

Deaf to cruelty
No violence on the streets
Zero tolerance
For Bullying

You see this is real humanity
It is like the five senses
You can taste, touch
Hear, feel and see

My Voice

Is drowning through the fan
It is like swimmers' ear
You not trying to hear
You just not listening

I whisper as the candle burns
I am in disbelief
I can't believe
What I hear
My voice deleted

My voice is put on mute
Pause
Because you not for the cause
I just dissolve
It's all a fog

It can make a sister angry
When she feels she is not being heard
It the word it's a verb
You heard
All confused so I am going to walk away dude

My words are beautiful
Listen to my voice
It makes angels sing
So poised
So polite

Please listen to my Voice you heard
It's like All lives Matter
Because it Matters
So precious
So true

It's rough around the edges
But shaped like a diamond
Humble as a hummingbird
Shallow as a whale
Listen to my words you heard

Empire State of Mind

The Empire state building reaches sky high
A sky away from infinity
To the top of Heavens
The view is magnificent

People look down or take a photo opt
Should your mind reach them type of heights?
Can you imagine if you did?
Would it be boundaries?
Would your mind reach the peak?

Is the mind cloudy as a raining day?
With each step there's a new dimension
Are you reaching the top?
Are you reaching the universe?
Where the neurons and stars converse

The mind is magnificent
It has many reasons and treasures
It is so powerful
WE only use 10 percent
It has a six sense

From head to toe
What you put in your mind use it wisely
Anything negative be mindful
Throw away the junk
You are a King or Queen
Develop a mind of character
The mind of an Empire
An Empire state of Mind

Just Be Real

If you got a story to tell just keep it real
Folks not trying to be nosey they just want to know the real deal
If you used drugs, had sex for money, pimped with a crack pipe in hand
Don't worry all have sinned

Demons all around
Lurking to devour in the midst it seems if you are in punching rounds
Real is you
It cannot be used by another soul
No not one ounce
So, tell your story for the next one that is hurt
If you have to tremble and shake do not make that mistake
Open your mouth and talk about you

Talk about the real and how you over came
It is you
The real in you

Do Not Touch

Do not touch my dreams
It is all up in my D.N.A
God planted my dreams
And it blossoms like flowers you see

Do not touch this dream
I fought so hard for
I will fight you for this
Blow to Blow, with a left and a right hook

Do not touch my dreams
Talent is its name
Hated with so much pain
This dream is locked up with chains

Do not touch this dream
Jesus died for me
And Rose three days later
So I can Rise, Rise, Rise

Do not touch my dreams
See it has been pruned
It has been beaten
Nevertheless, it is a blessing

Do not touch my dreams
It is glistening from within
No darkness on earth or hell can make it bend

Do not touch my dreams
I am going to hold on to it
Like rope it will not break
Because it is solid like a rock

Do not touch my dreams

Too much effort, blood, and sweat
To go down in flames
With arrow, darts, and spears

Do not touch my dreams
The slaves I know was
Beaten and hanged
I can do more than just being

Do not touch my dreams
You can lie
Shout what I will not be
But this dream has a shield

Do not touch my dreams
The rain falls
Too many times I walk alone
But each step I get closer to the throne
Do not touch my dreams
It has been shaken and even dropped
But this dream is like birth pains
Agony but so sweet

Do not touch my dreams
It has been beaten and punched
But the bruises are healing
The marks do not burn

Do not touch my dreams
Look out world
A flower has blossomed
And is not covered with dirt no more

Do not touch my dreams
But be thankful for my awesome
Because you
Cannot touch my dreams

Forever, Forever Romance

Is it always?
Is it forever?
Can it take a while?
Does it last?
Will forever be forever?

Is it short?
Is it long?
Can it be infinity?
Is forever eternity?
Can you chase it
Can it be a dream?

Is forever a fantasy?
Is it a lifestyle?
Can you turn the pages?
Like a romance novel
Is forever real?
Is it raw?
Forever, Forever Romance

Blessings

As you lay you down to sleep
Thank God for the blessings
He has kept you
Through happy times and sad days
God has kept you so be grateful
Blessings in so many ways
Financially, physically, and mentally
What God has for you is already mapped out and planned
Therefore, it is a blessing to be blessed throughout the mess
For be happy God has bestowed upon you so many
Blessings

Golden Gates

Bridges High and Low
Water rising with high tides
Folks walking across the bridge reminiscing

Traffic jams
Cars slowing down
While red station wagons are passing

The suns beaming
While couples are whale watching near the railing
The Golden gate bridge is glistening

Music is playing on the radio
Traffic still on a standstill
The only thing on people's mind is living golden

Leaving all obstacles at home while sitting in the sun
Children licking ice cream cones
Jill Scott's song in the stereo serenading
Life is Golden

Traffic jam stops
People drive ahead
Sun kissed lips
Because you know it's going to be golden as you drive ahead

Issa Flower

It became an idea from God
The faith of a mustard seed
All it need is a little dirt from the earth
A lot of water from the skies
Plenty of sunshine

After much cultivating, it became a beautiful flower
Maybe it was a daisy
It definitely was a rose
It was even much brighter a sunflower from a far

As time went past, the flower became more defined
The leaves became greener
The color of the flower became brighter
The flower became stronger with water
The overall appearance of the flower became magnificent

That Flower was I
Why?
Because Issa Flower always
Blooming

Rebirthed

It's been years since I have written with this pen…
Hands feel like dried up bones
Stained and tarnished
Drenched in blood

It withered away somehow
All attentions and hope were lost
It played hide and seek
And couldn't be found

It sat in tears these hands
Hopeless and confused
Waited on others dreams
To rise up and be intrigued

The stars in the sky did not shine in my mind
You see the brain did not function well
I felt full of shame
I was the one to blame

The eyes did not shed a tear
It could not even water a sparrow
The spirit could not be saved
No not a wreck like me

Then one day while eating Sundays best
All alone in the cold
God said get up child
It's time for a rebirth

God stated
And I looked
He said it again
"Get up child I have more work for you to do"

I was hesitant
Full of dismay
What God wanted with tired old me?
But I knew I had to obey

So, I stood up in that cold room
With no familiarity of life
I put one foot on the pavement
And never looked back

I stood up before the hands of time
I was not going to let this world take my mind
I counted the days to get out
Because I knew, I did not belong

That day finally came
I saw the light
I was given my belongings
And I stepped out to the light

The first day back in the real world I got a pink journal
I knew then I had to rebirth and write
Talk about my hurdles
In this hot pink diary

Not to mention
On the front pages of this diary
It's covered with golden flowers
It feels like bursting firecrackers

Issa flower always blooming
I will always have a story
A testimony or two
I have been rebirthed with my hands

I will always have a pen and paper
To let the words come out

I have a story
I have been rebirthed

Thank you

I would like to first say thank you to the Divine Jehovah who is with me at all times through my peaks and valleys. Jehovah has always thought of me as greatness and now I realize it. Thank you, Jehovah. I would like to thank my mother for always being by my side. To my dad, I cherish the special moments we have when I go home to visit you in Norfolk, Virginia. To my brother Joe Hagans, thanks for showing me higher wisdom and riding with me through the thick and thin...

To everyone who encouraged me through my mental breakdown with yellow flowers, (Chaneta). Sat and listened to my ranting words but left your job to come encouraged me anyway (Raynita Brinkley). To my aunt Elenora Battle who opened her home for me to stay for a while. Thank you to my aunt Doreatha Ross. You encouraged me and put living words in my soul and told me what I have in me, thank you. To all my aunts, uncles, cousins, and friends thank you for crossing my path there are no coincidences you're Earth Angels...

To Reverend Sheila Reid Dent, thank you for taking the time out to read my poems on Facebook and giving me my first platform to write a poem for a women's event. The poem went far in the hands of a book called: "Joyfully in his Care: Women living in all circumstances" ...

I would like to say thank you to my mentor, coach, and friend Andrenee Boothe for us crossing paths. Thank you for giving me a deadline to finish this book and encouraging me to love myself in the space I'm in right now. I'm so humble and glad to be in A Tribe Beautiful and the membership has been a beautiful and awakening experience...

To my Heavenly Angels both of my Grandmothers who went on to be with the Divine Doreatha Alexander and Annie Hagans for leaving a legacy and always being with me. I feel your presence every day. You both have given me extra strength. This book is dedicated to you both. Hugs and kisses from infinity and beyond...

To never forget anyone my hopes is to inspire anyone who comes within my path because I have been rebirthed. Let's keep the living thread going and inspire each other. We are not strangers to each other but alive and living abundantly. Choose you on your spiritual journey and the best of it all, choose love...

Thank you...

About the Author

Natashia Hagans was born in Portsmouth Virginia on August 13, 1978 and grew up in the District of Columbia and nearby in Landover Maryland. She has a bachelor's degree in Early Childhood Education and is currently teaching. Her passion is writing to inspire herself and others, she has published several poems showcased in newsletters and in a book called "Joyfully in his Care: Women living in all Circumstances". The most important thing Natashia Hagans wants people to know about her is that she is a masterpiece from the Divine
Natashia Hagans can be followed on Facebook, twitter, Instagram and her very own YouTube channel under (Natashia Hagans). You will be inspired.

Made in the USA
Middletown, DE
02 April 2021